BE A MAKER!

MAKER PROJECTS FOR KIDS WHO LOVE

ROBOTICS

JAMES BOW

CRABTREE
Publishing Company
www.crabtreebooks.com

Crabtree Publishing Company

www.crabtreebooks.com

Author: James Bow

Publishing plan research and development:
Reagan Miller

Editors: Sarah Eason and Harriet McGregor

Proofreaders: Nancy Dickmann, Petrice Custance

Editorial director: Kathy Middleton

Design: Paul Myerscough

Cover design: Emma DeBanks

Photo research: Rachel Blount

**Production coordinator and
Prepress techician:** Tammy McGarr

Print coordinator: Margaret Amy Salter

Consultant: Chris Stone

Production coordinated by Calcium Creative

Library and Archives Canada Cataloguing in Publication

Bow, James, 1972-, author
    Maker projects for kids who love robotics / James Bow.

(Be a maker!)
Includes index.
Issued in print and electronic formats.
ISBN 978-0-7787-2254-0 (bound).--
ISBN 978-0-7787-2266-3 (paperback).--
ISBN 978-1-4271-1721-2 (html)

    1. Robotics--Juvenile literature. 2. Robots--Juvenile litera-
ture. . Title.

TJ211.2.B68 2016   j629.8'92   C2015-907930-6
                                            C2015-907931-4

Library of Congress Cataloging-in-Publication Data

CIP available at the Library of Congress

Crabtree Publishing Company

www.crabtreebooks.com   1-800-387-7650

Printed in Canada/022016/MA20151130

Published in Canada
Crabtree Publishing
616 Welland Ave.
St. Catharines, Ontario
L2M 5V6

Published in the United States
Crabtree Publishing
PMB 59051
350 Fifth Avenue, 59th Floor
New York, New York 10118

Published in the United Kingdom
Crabtree Publishing
Maritime House
Basin Road North, Hove
BN41 1WR

Published in Australia
Crabtree Publishing
3 Charles Street
Coburg North
VIC, 3058

CONTENTS

TIME TO MAKE!

Look around you. Most things you see have been made by people. Everything from the chair you are sitting on, to the computer you are working at, has been made by either a person or a machine. And if it was made by a machine, then that machine was made by a person, somewhere down the line. Someone thought about it, and someone invented it.

MAKERS

Making things makes us who we are. It is why most of us live in houses and not in trees or caves. We built shelters. We built tools that made jobs easier. We turned these tools into machines that work for us. Recently, we have turned these machines into robots that can think for themselves.

But making is about more than just building things. Unlike most of the animals around us, we imagine and we create. We learn from our mistakes and grow through **experimentation**. And, most of all, we share our knowledge, so we can keep on improving what we make.

A lot of people, both students and professionals, are making the robots of tomorrow.

MAKING ROBOTS

In this book, we will be learning about robots. Robots were created because people experimented with machines that made work easier. They imagined, they created, they tested, they made mistakes, and they learned from those mistakes. They shared their knowledge and inspired others to build better robots. Robots were imagined centuries ago, and only started to do work in the 1900s. Today, robots are a big part of our lives.

MAKERSPACES

In this book, we will be learning from others who have changed the world by making things. We will follow their process of turning ideas into reality. Places where knowledge is shared and people build things are called **makerspaces**. In these places, we unleash our creativity and invent new ways of doing things, or **adapt** old ways to make new things. We learn and grow.

Makerspaces can be found anywhere, like your library, your community center, your school, or even on the Internet. By reading this book and trying some of the activities inside, you can create your own makerspace.

Monty, made by the robotics company Anybots, can pick things up, and is operated remotely by a person using a special glove.

Be a Maker!

What sort of robot would you build, if you could? What would you want it to do? Have you read anything about robots, or seen robots in action?

ROBOT INSPIRATION

When we first made tools to make our jobs easier, we imagined how great it would be if the tools could do all our work for us. That is when we started thinking about robots, or **automatons**.

MACHINES

In 200 BCE, a Greek mathematician named Ctesibius made a device called a *clepsydra*. This was a clock that used the weight of water to tell time. Ctesibius's idea of storing the energy of water and letting gravity do the work led to other innovations, such as using tension in a spring to power a clock. Eventually, we learned to burn coal to make steam and power engines, which kicked off the **Industrial Revolution**.

ROBOT REVOLUTION?

Once we created machines that could do some of our work, some people wondered if we could create machines that could be like us. In 1818, Mary Shelley published *Frankenstein*, a book about a scientist named Victor Frankenstein who used electricity to turn a corpse into a living being, similar to a robot. In 1920, Czech playwright Karel Čapek wrote *Rossum's Universal Robots*, which imagined people building millions of robots to do all the work. Čapek was the first to use the word "robot."

M·G·M PRESENTS
FORBIDDEN PLANET
AMAZING!

STARRING WALTER PIDGEON · ANNE FRANCIS · LESLIE NIELSEN
WITH WARREN STEVENS AND INTRODUCING ROBBY, THE ROBOT SCREEN PLAY BY CYRIL HUME BASED ON A STORY BY IRVING BLOCK AND ALLEN ADLER PHOTOGRAPHED IN EASTMAN COLOR
DIRECTED BY FRED McLEOD WILCOX · PRODUCED BY NICHOLAS NAYFACK in CINEMASCOPE AND COLOR

As shown by this movie poster, in the science fiction movies of the 1950s, robots were a very threatening presence.

At first, these stories did not end well. Shelley's Frankenstein created an uncontrollable monster. Čapek's robots replaced the human race. Starting in the 1950s, science fiction writers like Isaac Asimov helped change things by writing stories about how robots and humans could work together.

ROBOTS BECOME REAL

Meanwhile, machines were getting more complex. In 1948, a British scientist named William Grey Walter designed the first robot that could move on its own. By 1961, robotic arms were used to produce goods in hours that would take human workers weeks.

People feared robots could replace human workers and put everyone out of work. But robots also made lives better, manufacturing goods like automobiles, televisions, and computers so cheaply that more people could afford to buy them.

ASIMO, manufactured by Honda, is the first robot to walk on its own. It is being designed to be useful around the home.

Be a Maker!

Isaac Asimov's "Three Laws of Robotics," a set of rules about robots found in his science fiction books, were a safety device to ensure the robots in his stories always obeyed humans and didn't attempt to destroy their creators. These laws don't actually exist, but they helped people stop thinking of robots as a threat. Why do you think people were so afraid of robots in the past? Should they have been?

WHAT IS A ROBOT?

A robot is a machine that is more than just a tool. Unlike tools, robots can work **independently**. They need a power supply to give them the energy to do work and they are **sensitive**. This means that they respond to changes in their environment and do things based on what these changes tell them.

ROBOT OR NOT?

So, a robot is a machine. A toaster is also a machine. Is a toaster a robot? In some ways a toaster is a robot. A toaster has a sensor that responds to the environment around it. When the sensor is hot enough, it pops up the toast. But a toaster does not work independently. It needs a human to put in the bread and press down the lever to turn it on.

UNIMATE

The earliest robots were simple. Unimate, the first industrial robot, was a mechanical arm that picked up parts from a car assembly line and welded them onto larger parts. Unimate amazed people so much that its designers were invited onto *The Tonight Show* in 1961. There, the designers made Unimate knock a golf ball into a cup, pour a drink, and wave an orchestra baton. Since then, makers have improved robots, making them do more complex tasks.

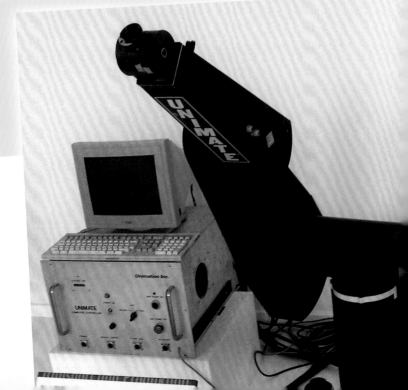

Unimate 500 Puma, built in 1983, was an industrial robot controlled by the computer beside it.

EYES, EARS, AND BRAINS

Like a person, a robot has sensors that receive data and transmit signals about the robot's environment. They are like our eyes and ears, although robot sensors can also sense heat and pressure, as well as light and sound. Robots have **actuators**, which are gears, motors, and springs. They act as the robot's "muscles," making it move. They also have a central processing unit, which uses programming language to tell it how to respond to what the sensors are saying. This is the robot's brain.

Today's robots have complex software, with millions of lines of **code** (see pages 24–25).

The robot Martian lander *Opportunity* was designed to work on Mars, a planet which humans cannot travel to yet.

Makers and Shakers

Ada Lovelace

Ada Lovelace (1815–1852) studied logic and mathematics. When she was 28 years old, she helped British mathematician Charles Babbage come up with the idea of the Analytical Engine. This proposed machine could do calculations and store numbers in its memory. Lovelace wrote the first **algorithm**—a set of instructions for the machine to carry out—which is thought to be the world's first computer program.

ROBOT BLOOD AND NERVES

A robot needs energy or power to work. Humans could provide that energy, moving the parts to get the robot functioning, but that does not save much work. Robots are only useful if they can do tasks on their own, so their power supply must work without people having to maintain it all the time.

ENERGY

The first automated machines used gravity and the flow of water to do work. Other machines stored energy in tightened springs. The energy was then released gradually, allowing the robot to do work. The stored energy in a tightened spring or in stored water is known as **potential energy**. When the spring or the water start to move, it is called **kinetic energy**.

Energy can also be passed as electricity through wires. This uses power from a source, such as a battery, which moves through a wire to an electrical device, such as a motor. The motor will only move when the electricity flows. For this to happen, you need a complete **circuit**.

This Japanese Karakuri was an automaton made in the 1800s. It can serve tea, and it is powered by a wound spring.

CIRCUITS

In a complete circuit, a second wire runs back from the motor to a different contact of the battery. This allows the electricity to flow. The electricity wants to get from one end of the battery to the other, but it can only do so by moving through the wires, and it can only do that by pushing through the motor and making it work. Cut the circuit, and the electricity no longer flows. Electricity helps make sensors work. When the sensors detect changes to the robot's environment, this may cause another circuit to be completed. This could deliver a jolt of electricity to a switch, completing a circuit and making the motor run.

Just as blood transmits energy to various parts of the human body, and nerve cells send signals between our brains and sensors all over our bodies, wires inside a robot send out energy and transmit information that help the robot move and respond.

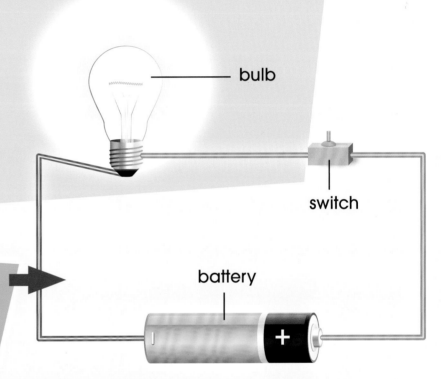

bulb

switch

battery

In this circuit, when the switch is closed, electricity flows from the battery, through the wires, and lights the bulb.

Be a Maker!

All robots need energy to work. When designing a robot, makers must choose a power source. Imagine you are designing a robot. Is it better to plug a robot into an electric socket or operate it with a battery? Think about the pros and cons of both choices.

INSPIRED BY NATURE

Designers who look at different sources of inspiration sometimes build robots that can do jobs much better than those designed to move like humans.

IMITATING HUMANS

Early robots looked like humans or parts of humans. Robot arms bent like human arms, with elbows, shoulders, and fingers to grab or poke. Robot limbs were stiff and solid, powered by electricity, gears, and motors. While all of this made the robots strong, it also made them less able to perform delicate tasks.

FESTO

Recently, a German robotics company named Festo invented a robotic arm made out of flexible plastic tubes. The makers were inspired by the way an elephant could grab and lift objects with its flexible trunk. The company discovered that by filling some of the tubes with air, they could control the stiffness of the robotic arm. Filling different tubes allowed them to twist and turn the arm in many directions. The hands took inspiration from the way a fish's tail curls back to one side when it is pushed to the other side. Using this type of mechanism, the robot's flexible plastic fingers can wrap around and clasp **fragile** objects without breaking them.

Octopuses, squid, and jellyfish swim better than humans do, so effective swimming robots are built using similar forms.

ONE BRAIN, MANY ROBOTS

The idea of using designs from the natural world to make robots is called **biomimicry**. A robot built to walk like a human will have difficulty walking over uneven ground just as humans do. A robot that is built to move like a cat or dog, however, will move easily over uneven ground just as these animals can. Similarly, who says one robot has to do all the work? If we can split the brain functions of a robot to a bunch of smaller robots that communicate with each other and work together, we can create swarms of insect-like robots that can do tasks that larger single robots could not.

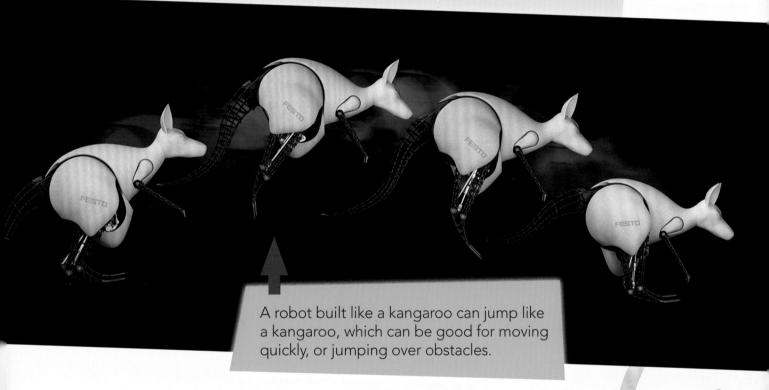

A robot built like a kangaroo can jump like a kangaroo, which can be good for moving quickly, or jumping over obstacles.

Be a Maker!

The newest robots can rewrite their code in order to learn. They learn by making mistakes. They are able to predict what is supposed to happen, analyze what did happen, figure out the difference between the two, and try a new way to solve the problem. Is this similar to the way you learn? What other ways can you learn? How might a robot do it?

MAKE IT!
A ROBOT HAND

Now that we have learned what makes a robot a robot, the time has come to make our own! Try making a robot hand.

YOU WILL NEED
- Scissors
- Cardboard
- Ruler
- Tape
- Rubber bands
- String
- Straws
- Pen

1
- Cut a piece of cardboard into a square, about 5 inches (13 cm) by 5 inches (13 cm). This will be your robot's palm.
- Cut four pieces of cardboard about 1 inch (2.5 cm) wide and 3.5 inches (9 cm) long. These will be the fingers.

2
- Cut your robot fingers into three equal parts, then join them back together with a single piece of tape along one side. These will be the joints of your robot hand.
- Line up the fingers with your robot hand's palm and tape them to the palm.

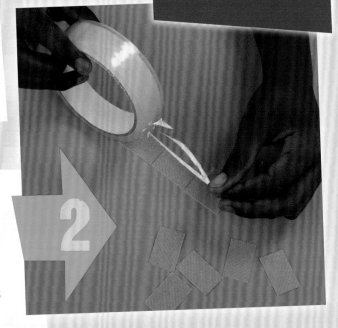

3
- Turn the hand over. Cut four sections of rubber band, each 5 inches (12 cm) long.
- Place a piece of rubber band along each of your robot's fingers.
- Tape each band down on both sides of each joint, making sure the bands will not slip.

- Turn your hand over, so the rubber bands are on the bottom.
- Cut three pieces of string, each 14 inches (35 cm) long.
- Tape one end of each string over the end of each finger.
- Cut straws into 12 pieces, each 0.75 inches (2 cm) long.
- Put four pieces of the straw over the string on each finger.
- Tape each piece of straw to the middle of each finger section, leaving one piece to tape onto the palm.

4

5

- Pull on each string and see how the fingers move.
- Can you pick up a light object, such as a paper ball, with your robot hand?
- Can you make the hand wave?

CONCLUSION

Do not expect to succeed on the first try. Makers learn from their mistakes. Share your experience with others and listen to what they have to say. With their feedback you can revise your plans and make them better.

Make It Even Better!

Can you make the hand stronger? What happens if you add more fingers or a thumb? Are there ways you can make it easier to pull each string? How many different versions do you imagine robot makers went through as they improved the design of their robots?

WALKING ROBOTS

Although the first robots moved, they could not travel from one location to another. Getting the robots to move from place to place makes them more useful. However, making robots walk by themselves is very complicated. Many different parts of a robot's body must **coordinate** and move at the same time without causing the robot to fall over.

LEGS

Early robot designers found that robots have an easier time walking if they have a lower center of gravity, which means that most of the robot's weight is closer to the ground. A stable base also helps.

But why use legs at all? Our cars drive on wheels, so why not robots? Robots are designed for specific purposes. So if a robot needs to climb it will likely be made with legs because legs are ideal for this movement. Lifting a leg up a sheer cliff face and gaining a foothold, gives an advantage over wheels on rough **terrain**.

Atla is designed to help in search and rescue operations by shutting off valves, opening doors, and operating equipment in places that are too hot or too full of smoke for humans to work.

BALANCE

Robots that rely on many legs and a low center of gravity can be heavy and slow. Companies such as Boston Dynamics are designing robots that can walk by themselves. The computers in the robots can work quickly enough to handle all of the processes involved in taking a step. **Gyroscopes** send messages to a computer brain telling it how all its parts are balanced. The computer then sends messages back to the legs to move. It constantly rechecks itself to make sure it is not losing balance.

One of Boston Dynamics' robots is known as BigDog, and it takes some inspiration from the way a dog walks in order to carry loads over uneven ground. A new robot, named the Cheetah, mimics the fastest land animal to run at speeds of up to 30 miles (48 km) per hour.

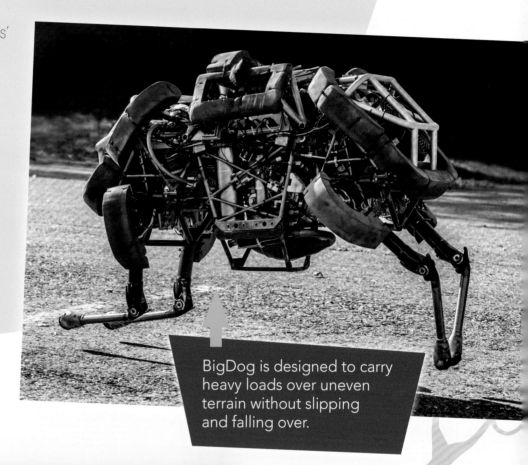

BigDog is designed to carry heavy loads over uneven terrain without slipping and falling over.

Makers and Shakers

Yaya Lu

Australian Yaya Lu (born 1997) was only 16 when she came up with an idea that would allow people who are paralyzed and unable to move their arms or legs to control their wheelchairs using voice commands. Yaya presented her research paper to the Biomedical Engineering International Conference and was awarded the prestigious Gold CREST Award.

DIFFERENT TOOLS, DIFFERENT TASKS

People design robots to perform specific jobs. This accounts for the different kinds of robots in our world today. For example, bomb disposal robots must be heavy and sturdy to withstand explosions. **Drones** are designed to fly like helicopters or planes depending on whether the drone needs to hover in one spot or fly quickly from place to place.

ROBOTS IN SPACE!

From the ocean floor to distant planets, different robots are designed for different environments. Robot landers sent to Mars such as *Spirit, Curiosity*, and *Opportunity* were specially designed to move around their environment. Their "legs" are six wheels that keep them stable on uneven ground, with special treads to grip the sandy surface. Their "arms" have drills to cut into rock and analyze materials. They have cameras to study the rock, watch where the rover is going, and take pictures. The Martian rovers also have solar power panels but robots like *New Horizons*, which visited Pluto in 2015, were too far from the Sun for solar panels to work. Instead, these explorer robots use a **nuclear battery** to keep them going.

The robot *Opportunity* arrived on Mars on January 25, 2004. It has traveled more than 25 miles (40 km) across the red planet, exploring and sending back data.

DESIGNING ROBOTS

One way to improve robot designs is to challenge designers to compete. One such competition is the RoboCup. Since 1997, university students from around the world have been designing robots that can play soccer. Robots from different countries compete against each other in a soccer tournament—just like the World Cup.

Another competition is the DARPA Grand Challenge, in which teams of university researchers and robotics manufacturers design cars that can drive themselves over a long and difficult course without human input. The FIRST robotics competition brings together teams of high school students to work together to design robots to meet a challenge set by the organizers. In 2015, the competition was called Recycle Rush. Competitors had to build robots that could stack recycling totes and collect trash.

These robots were the Australian team's entry in the 2010 RoboCup in Singapore.

Be a Maker!

Makers learn and improve their designs by sharing their ideas with others. Does competing against others contribute to this? How might the competition angle help people improve their design in ways that sharing might not?

MAKE IT!
INTRUDER ALARM

Some robots sense the world around them, and most contain an electrical circuit. Follow this project to make an intruder alarm that contains an electric circuit.

YOU WILL NEED
- Aluminum foil
- 2 pieces of cardboard, 6 inches (15 cm) by 5 inches (12.5 cm)
- Tape
- 3 pieces of plastic-coated copper wire, each 12 inches (30 cm) long
- Wire strippers
- An electric buzzer
- A 9 volt battery
- A rectangular section of bubble wrap, about 5 inches (12.5 cm) by 4 inches (10 cm)
- Scissors

1

- Wrap aluminum foil over one side of each cardboard square, taping it at the back.
- Using wire strippers, carefully remove around 1 inch (2.5 cm) of the plastic coating from both ends of all three wires.
- Tape one wire to the center of one foil-wrapped square. Do not put tape over the copper part of the wire. This part must be exposed.
- Repeat this step with the other foil-wrapped square. <u>Make sure that each wire is taped in the center of each square.</u>

2

- Take the loose end of one wire and twist the copper around one of the buzzer's connections.
- Tape the loose end of the second wire to the positive terminal of your battery.
- Tape one end of the third wire to the negative terminal of the battery.
- Twist the other end of the third wire to the other connector on your buzzer.

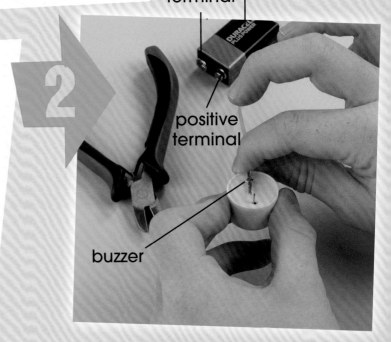

battery

negative terminal

positive terminal

buzzer

3

- Using scissors, cut a rectangular hole in the center of the bubble wrap. The hole should be around the size of a quarter.
- Tape the bubble wrap onto one of the foil-wrapped squares, as shown left. Make sure that the exposed copper wire can be seen through the hole in the bubble wrap.

- Stack the two cardboard pieces together with the wires facing each other. The bubble wrap should keep the wires from touching.

4

CONCLUSION

Pushing on the center of the cardboard should press the wires together. This completes the circuit and sets off the buzzer. You can now hide your intruder alarm under a mat in front of your bedroom door, where someone stepping on it will set off the alarm.

Make It Even Better!

What other devices can you attach to this battery that can be activated by completing the circuit? Where else could you place this alarm to detect intruders?

WORKING WITH PEOPLE

Robots have done a lot of work for people, and now robots are working with people. Some do tasks for the elderly, such as bringing food and reminding them to take their medications, which helps elderly people live independently longer.

MEDICAL ROBOTS

In certain hospitals, robots like the Aethon TUG are already moving medication, food, and linens from one part of the hospital to another. These robots never tire, and they can handle low-skilled tasks, allowing hospitals to spend more money hiring nurses and doctors. Other robots can visit patients with a two-way video screen, allowing a specialized doctor from anywhere in the world to consult with a patient.

THE EXO-SUIT

Robotic exo-suits are mechanical suits that people wear to help them lift heavy objects. The suit is worn around the body, like armor. Joints allow the wearer to move, while the metal **struts** and **hydraulic** muscles provide extra strength. The military are researching exo-suits to help soldiers walk while carrying heavy gear without getting tired. Medical researchers are also looking at using exo-suits to help people who are paralyzed. The exo-suit would help the person to stand up and walk.

Exo-suits could one day help paralyzed people walk by providing mechanical support for their legs and hips.

Robots are already being used as personal helpers. They are often human-like in appearance.

In the future, an exo-suit's computer could read signals from a person's brain, allowing a paralyzed person to control their exo-suit as they used to control their own body.

HITCHBOT

All of this means that people are working more often with robots, which can be difficult if people are not comfortable with robots. To deal with this, designers try to make robots look non-threatening. This does not always work. In 2014, scientists at McMaster and Ryerson Universities in Canada designed HitchBOT. This robot looked human-like and had a tablet computer, a GPS locator, and a camera. People were encouraged to take HitchBOT with them on a journey across Canada. After successfully crossing Canada and then Germany in 2014, with dozens of people having their photograph taken with the robot, HitchBOT visited the United States. Unfortunately, after traveling to Boston and New York City, HitchBOT was destroyed by vandals in Philadelphia.

Be a Maker!

How would you design a robot to help people? What would you have the robot do? What would you do to make sure people were comfortable with your robot?

MAKING ROBOTS THINK

The first science fiction writers wrote about a future in which robots were so smart they could overpower humans. Fortunately, this is not the case yet! Robots are machines that have computers for "brains." These computers are given instructions by humans that tell them what to do—which means that we control them.

THE TURING TEST

Alan Turing (1912–1954) was a British mathematician and computer scientist who helped build a computing machine that broke the German's secret codes during World War II (1939–1945). In 1948, he investigated whether a computer could think like a human. He designed the Turing Test, where if a computer can convince a human that he is speaking to a human, the computer is said to be intelligent.

Today, robots still will not do anything unless we write the code that tells them what to do. Robots and computers use a machine language, which is a series of numbers. This machine language is called code. It tells the computer and robot what parts to move, when to move those parts, and so on.

TOPIO is a robot that can play ping-pong. Its computer "brain" learns to improve its skills while playing.

LEARNING

Computers can figure out numbers faster than humans, but to build a robot that can beat a human at chess, we need to write code to tell a computer what chess is, how the pieces move, and even what it means to win. Deep Blue, the machine that beat the chessmaster Garry Kasparov in 1997, was built by IBM and programmed by dozens of people, including other chess masters. It took 12 years of hard work by humans writing thousands of lines of code to get the computer to beat the best human. A more challenging task is programming a computer to learn. In 2011, IBM built a computer named Watson that used a large database and speech recognition to understand the questions in the trivia show *Jeopardy!* It took on the game's best players, and won.

Building a computer brain that can play chess is one thing. Building a robot arm to move chess pieces is a far more difficult challenge.

Be a Maker!

While Watson did well on *Jeopardy!*, it is actually designed to help doctors identify illnesses and suggest treatments. How do you think having a team of Watsons might help doctors in the future?

ROBOT REVOLUTION

One hundred years ago, robots were nothing but science fiction, but fiction gave people ideas. People took these ideas, made designs, and built these designs into **prototypes**. Prototypes are early attempts at a project. People tested their prototypes, shared their results with others, and learned from their mistakes. The achievements and **collaboration** of past makers has led to the robot technology we have today.

BE A ROBOT MAKER

You already have the tools to make robots. The experiments in this book teach you how robots move, and demonstrate how they can be powered, but why stop there? There are toys out there that help you build robots. You can put together the frame and gears, and attach a power supply to make them move. There are resources online that can teach you how to program a robot.

Schools and universities often run robotics competitions, challenging students to learn more about robots and build better robotic designs.

COLLABORATION

The main thing that takes robots out of the imagination and into the real world is collaboration. People work together in makerspaces, sharing ideas, helping each other understand what works, what does not work, and why. Robot makers often work in teams. Sometimes the teams stretch through time as people read ideas written down long ago, and are inspired to then try their own designs.

BUILD YOUR TEAM

If you want to learn more about making robots, look around in your community for a robotics club you can join. Develop your own ideas and experiment with prototypes. Reach out to friends and share your ideas. Compete in robot challenges. Listen and learn. Most importantly, have fun!

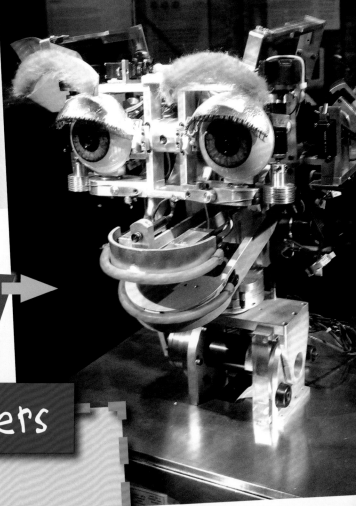

Kismet was designed by MIT to recognize emotions and copy them in return.

Makers and Shakers

Cynthia Breazeal

Cynthia Breazeal (born in 1967) is a pioneer in robot–human interaction. She creates robots that react to humans in ways humans understand. Her most famous creation is Leonardo, a furry creature with a camera and nearly 60 motors to track movement and imitate human expressions. Leonardo can follow people's fingers and look at what people are pointing at, allowing it to better interact with a person by noticing what the person is paying attention to.

MAKE IT!
SOLAR-POWERED ROBOT

Now that we have worked on different parts of a robot, we can put our knowledge together and create an actual robot powered by solar energy.

YOU WILL NEED

- An old solar-powered garden light
- Scissors
- A 1.5 volt low-speed DC motor (you can buy these from an electronics store or upcycle an old one from an old DVD player)
- An old CD or DVD
- Sticky tack
- A clear plastic dome recycled from a drink cup
- Electrician's tape
- Clear tape
- A flashlight

1

- Take apart the garden light, removing any batteries or capacitors. You should see two wires running from the solar panel to a circuit board.
- Cut away the circuit board, leaving as much of the wires attached to the solar panel as possible.

2

- Take a CD or a DVD and push the shaft of the motor through the hole.
- Attach the shaft to the CD with sticky tack.

3

- Put the wires from the solar panel through the hole in the clear plastic dome and attach them to the contact points of the motor.
- Seal with electrician's tape.

- Center the clear plastic dome on the CD or DVD over the motor.
- Attach the dome to the CD or DVD with clear tape.

4

5

- Place your robot (on its sticky tack base end) on a smooth, flat surface and shine a bright light on it. The motor should spin, causing your robot to spin and dance.

CONCLUSION

Now that you know how to power robots and make them move, what other robots can you make? What other materials can you use? What can you make your robots do? The opportunities are endless!

Make It Even Better!

What would happen if you added more power? With these supplies, what else can you make that will move? What other objects can you make robots from, and what can you make them do? Keep trying new ideas and enjoy your robots!

GLOSSARY

actuators Devices that take energy—usually energy created by air, electricity, or liquid—and change it into movement

adapt To change to better cope with the environment or conditions

algorithm A set of instructions followed by a computer to achieve a certain goal

automatons Machines that imitate human beings

biomimicry Copying ideas or designs found in nature

circuit A closed loop of wire, usually connecting an energy source and a device such as a light bulb, through which electricity can flow

code A set of instructions a computer or a robot has to follow

collaboration Working with other people toward a common goal

coordinate Work together at the same time and in the right way

drones Robots that can fly, either by themselves or by remote control, and perform tasks while in the air

experimentation The process of trying out ideas

fragile Easy to break; delicate

gyroscopes Spinning discs held within frames. The spinning disc resists changes to its orientation (the direction in which it points)

hydraulic To be operated by water pressure

independently Doing things without another's help or control

Industrial Revolution A time of significant growth and changes to industries in the 1700s and 1800s

kinetic energy Energy that an object has while it is moving

makerspaces Places where makers gather to innovate, share resources, and learn from one another

nuclear battery A battery that gets its energy from the decay of radioactive material

potential energy Energy that an object has, but has not yet used, such as a rock on top of a steep hill that is not yet rolling down

prototypes Early attempts to build a design, allowing you to test your design ideas, and learn how to improve them

sensitive Able to see, hear, or feel what is around you, and react to it

struts Bars designed to resist pressure

terrain A stretch of ground, and how it rises and falls

LEARNING MORE

BOOKS

Ceceri, Kathy, and Samuel Carbaugh. *Robotics*. Nomad, 2012.

Freedman, Jeri. *Robots through History*. Rosen Central, 2011.

Peppas, Lynn. *Robotics*. Crabtree, 2014.

Stewart, Melissa. *Robots*. National Geographic Society, 2014.

WEBSITES

Click through the incredible array of new robots and watch movies of them at:
www.bostondynamics.com/index.html

There are links to building every kind of robot imaginable at:
www.instructables.com/id/Your-First-Robot

Click "Do This Activity" at the following website to visit the Robotics Lab and build your own virtual robot:
kidsahead.com/subjects/1-robotics/activities/26

Learn about the history of robots, artificial intelligence, the jobs robots do, and how to build a robot at:
www.razorrobotics.com